Roy
Lichtenstein

D1430584

By Diane Waldman

RIZZOLI ART SERIES

Series Editor: Norma Broude

Roy

Lichtenstein

(b. 1923)

In 1961 Roy Lichtenstein appropriated the image of a girl tossing a beach ball in the air from an advertisement in *The New York Times* promoting a resort called Mount Airy Lodge. The ad was attractive to the artist because the figure looked like a cliché, a bit of cheesecake like Betty Grable, who survived the Second World War to become a pinup in newspaper, magazine, and television commercials. The comely figure in the ad beckons to her readers, selling them the delights of honeymooning in the Poconos. Lichtenstein borrowed this bathing-suited figure and used her as his model for *Girl with Ball* (plate 1). Lichtenstein transformed her from her commonplace origins in the media into an emblem of American culture. She took her place alongside such iconoclastic figures as Edouard Manet's *Olympia*, Pablo Picasso's *Demoiselles d'Avignon*, and Willem de Kooning's *Woman*, a vernacular subject who found her way into the canon of art. An archetype as American as apple pie, she became an appropriate replacement in the new American painting for the European and American models who preceded her. As a new image in painting, she was an awesome accomplishment. That she would become a durable fixture in advertising and an icon in painting was beyond the realm of the artist's imagination in 1961, although he clearly understood the appeal of his subject in a consumer culture. That he was able to convert this unlikely figure into an image attractive to an audience accustomed to a utopian art of ideal form is testimony to his singular achievement as an artist.

Girl with Ball was one of a number of "comic-strip" paintings Lichtenstein brought into the Leo Castelli Gallery in the fall of 1961. He showed the paintings to Ivan Karp, then director of the gallery, whose reaction was one of immediate enthusiasm. Although Castelli was also intrigued with the work, he said he needed some time to think about the paintings and suggested Lichtenstein return in a few weeks. When he did, Castelli offered him a one-man show. The exhibition, which opened on February 10, 1962, met with a mixed reception. Many of Lichtenstein's friends and fellow artists loved the work, as did a small but influential group of collectors. The majority of the art world, however, was scandalized. To an audience whose vision was linked to that of the Abstract Expressionists, the very notion of comic-strip painting was anathema: Pop Art was the crass enemy of everything they stood for. Abstract Expressionism represented an era in painting when such artists as Jackson Pollock, Willem de Kooning, Mark Rothko, Barnett Newman, and

Clyfford Still evolved a body of work in which the canvas became the arena for a heroic series of actions or meditations. Pop Art, on the other hand, or "popular art," was a term first used in 1958 by the British critic Lawrence Alloway to describe a London-based group of artists, writers, and architects, whose work was inspired by such contemporary forms of mass culture as comic strips, commercials, Hollywood movies, science fiction, and pop music. Alloway later applied his term also to New York–based artists who, like Lichtenstein, shared many of the same interests as their British counterparts.

Although Lichtenstein practiced a form of Abstract Expressionism briefly in the late 1950s, he soon began to add abstracted cartoons to his paintings. He liked the idea of putting a nonserious subject into a serious art context. By 1961 these images became the nucleus of his work. Like Andy Warhol, James Rosenquist, George Segal, and Claes Oldenburg, each of whom was working independently, Lichtenstein sought to represent the external world of the consumer rather than the internal world of the subconscious. As an extroverted art replaced introspection, the methods of the media and its appeal to a mass market were seized upon by this group of artists, for whom abstraction no longer had meaning. As Lichtenstein noted in 1963: "Everybody was hanging everything. It was almost acceptable to hang a dripping paint rag, everybody was accustomed to this. The one thing everybody hated was commercial art." [1] Although Lichtenstein insisted he was not being critical of Abstract Expressionism, he went on to note that he was "anti-contemplative, anti-nuance, anti-getting-away-from-the-tyranny-of-the-rectangle, anti-movement and light, anti-mystery, anti-paint-quality, anti-Zen, and anti all of those brilliant ideas of preceding movements which everybody understands so thoroughly." In protesting a whole range of ideas that he found neither provocative nor profound, Lichtenstein verbalized the frustration of a younger generation of artists for whom action painting had become stalemated. In reaction to the Abstract Expressionists' esoteric declarations, Lichtenstein declared an art that was its opposite. He chose the cartoon partly for its value as sensational subject matter and partly because he liked the friction between the commonplace and fine art. It was this feature of his work, the notorious marriage of low art subject and high art style, that first brought him to prominence in 1961 and for which he justly became celebrated in the late 1960s.

Lichtenstein chose to mirror the world of the middle-class consumer, but he was quick to point out that his work "is actually different from comic strips in that every mark is really in a different place, however slight the difference seems to some. The difference is often not great, but it is crucial . . . the comics have shapes but there has been no effort to make them intensely unified. The purpose is different, one intends to depict and I intend to unify." [2] Lichtenstein used this particular subject matter in order to comment on it. It provided him with a way of making an anti-art statement that he could then transform into art. A comparison of *Girl with Ball* with the ad from which she was taken gives ample evidence of the distinction. Lichtenstein altered the rounded figure in the photograph into a flat two-dimensional form, which he enlarged so he could crop it dramatically at top and bottom. He retained the reference to the benday process, a method of reproduction that uses line engraving o create tints or areas of shading made up of dots, from the original ad, but used it as a way of emphasizing the figure's formal qualities. He also eliminated the lengthy message that accompanied the figure, and in place of the original photograph he used the primary colors found in advertising. *Girl with Ball*, the first in a long line of images of women the artist painted, is an enduring emblem of American pop culture. She is a femme fatale and the wholesome girl next door, a fixture from the 1940s and 1950s who continues to represent the ideal female in a male-dominated society.

Roy Lichtenstein was born in 1923 into a middle-class family in New York City. He grew up on Manhattan's West Side and attended a private high school from the eighth through the twelfth grades. As a teenager he began to paint and draw on his own and attended many jazz concerts at the Apollo Theater in Harlem. He also frequented jazz clubs on Fifty-second Street and painted a series of portraits of jazz musicians inspired by Picasso's famous depictions of musical performers. In 1939 he took summer classes at the Art Students League and studied with the American Regionalist painter Reginald Marsh. When he graduated from high school in 1940 he decided to further his studies by enrolling in the fine arts program at Ohio State University. There he studied with Professor Hoyt L. Sherman, whom he credits with teaching him about theories of visual perception and formal organization. Sherman de-emphasized the importance of relating the object to the model from which it was drawn. Instead he stressed the importance of the object and the need to make each mark work in relationship to the mark next to it. From his concepts Lichtenstein developed his own theories of form.

World War II interrupted Lichtenstein's studies, and he was drafted into the army. His tour of duty lasted from 1943 to 1945. When he returned to the States, he went back to Ohio to finish his studies under the G.I. Bill. He taught at Ohio State until 1951 and worked at a series of odd jobs until 1957, when he began to teach at the State University of New York in Oswego. In 1960 he joined the faculty of Douglass College, Rutgers University, New Jersey. Through Allan Kaprow, who also taught fine art at Rutgers, Lichtenstein met Oldenburg, Jim Dine, Segal, and Lucas Samaras. Lichtenstein became interested in performance art and "Happenings," a term invented by Kaprow for performances which, influenced by the music of John Cage and the dances of Merce Cunningham and Paul Taylor, emphasized the importance of improvisation and capitalized on chance effects. In the Happenings artists shared the stage with overblown objects and other commonplace items. These props soon began to figure prominently in the work of many of the Pop artists. It was not long after he saw the Happenings that Lichtenstein began his first Pop paintings.

In still life paintings of 1961 and 1962, such as *Black Flowers* (plate 2), Lichtenstein established one of the main themes of his work. He selected a crass commercial subject and painted a still life in a manner that recalls the original ad, but he reconfigured it into a bold new image. The flowers and their container have been flattened into a shorthand sequence of lines and benday dots, placed on a tabletop—which is tipped foward in a manner worthy of the way in which Paul Cézanne foreshortened his tabletop and

arrangements of fruit—and secured to the picture plane by a wall of benday dots. In using black and white as his only colors and screening several areas with benday dots, Lichtenstein deliberately neutralized the volumes in the paintings. He also forsook the look of a hand-painted image for a mass-produced one. It is tempting to see in this painting references to the French Post-Impressionist Georges Seurat and his fellow Pointillists. Lichtenstein's use of commercial benday dots reminds us of the Pointillist's use of a system of dots to approximate the way in which colors blend together in nature when viewed from a certain distance. The artifice in Lichtenstein's still life shares with the artifice of the Pointillists the issue of perception. Theirs was a reconstruction of nature using a system derived from natural phenomena; Lichtenstein's is a reconstruction of a still life derived not from a natural form but from the mechanical forms of newspaper reproduction. Lichtenstein found the image for *Black Flowers* in a newspaper ad. He liked the image because "it seemed the opposite of the romantic, heartfelt, spilling-your-guts-out posture of Abstract Expressionism. The reproductions in newspapers were usually done by artists with very little training and they had a plodding and unartistic appearance. Also, anything printed looked fake or spurious and it wasn't really art."[3] This unartistic quality appealed to him, as did the fact that he could make an unartistic subject into a painting.

1. *Golf Ball*. 1962. Oil on canvas, 32 x 32 ".
Private Collection

Lichtenstein's striking use of a black-and-white palette is a feature of other paintings of the period, among them *Golf Ball* and *Portrait of Madame Cézanne* (figs. 1 and 2), and may refer to the black-and-white paintings created by Abstract Expressionists Willem de Kooning, Franz Kline, and Ad Reinhardt in the 1940s and 1950s. In *Golf Ball*, Lichtenstein makes explicit reference to the early abstractionist Piet Mondrian by emulating his system of structuring nature into a sequence of plus and minus signs. The hooked black marks and the decisive black outline delineate the shape of the golf ball, a common enough object, at the same time they recall the distinctive nature of Mondrian's oeuvre. *Portrait of Madame Cézanne*, on the other hand, is a painting based on the art historian Earl Loran's diagram of Cézanne's portrait, which was first published in 1943. Lichtenstein felt that the notion of diagramming the forms in Cézanne's painting was a total oversimplification of the art, and it amused him to make this the subject of a painting. In *George Washington* (plate 3), Lichtenstein uses the

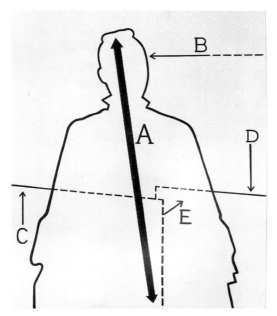

2. *Portrait of Madame Cézanne.* 1962.
Magna on canvas, 7 x 6". Private Collection,
New York

unartistic drawing style of the comic strips to convert a formidable subject into an image that looks like a reproduction. His image refers to the image of the president engraved on a dollar bill as well as to heroic portraits painted by artists such as Gilbert Stuart. By using the mechanical process of reproduction in his painting, Lichtenstein is able to remind the viewer of the dollar bill, but because the portrait is authoritative and its subject conventional, he can also recall "official" portraiture. Thus Lichtenstein's figure of the first president of the United States is as imposing as any "official" portrait and as absurd as his caricature on a dollar bill: an apt description of the nature of official art in our culture. In his painting of George Washington, Lichtenstein created a stunning portrait from a sequence of spare black-and-white shapes and added a series of red benday dots to the face to simulate the color in the Stuart painting. His use of the ubiquitous benday dot and black and white to evoke simultaneously volume and flatness is one of the more astounding feats of his early work, as is his ability to convert a stereotype into a compelling image.

Lichtenstein's disparate subjects share many things in common: whether cartoon or still life, Picasso or George Washington, they are transposed through the language of advertising into images in the medium of art. The new icon and the new perception that result are Lichtenstein's gift to art.

Lichtenstein derived his popular imagery from a number of sources, including bubble-gum wrappers, animated cartoons, the Manhattan Yellow Pages, such D.C. comic books as "Teen Romance" and "Our Army at War," and magazine and newspaper illustrations. Since all subject matter was up for grabs, he also drew on the art of Picasso and Mondrian to work from because their style lent itself to re-creation. His subjects included a mix of consumer products, like refrigerators, washing machines, and stoves, and commercial items, like sponges, tires, golf balls, engagement rings, balls of twine, pies, frankfurters, and sneakers. He redrew the small-scale images from the original advertisements into equally small sketches. When he was satisfied with his version of the original he made a color sketch, which he projected onto a canvas by means of an opaque projector. He again redrew the drawing on the canvas, applied a series of

benday dots and primary colors, and finished an image with heavy black outlines. Lichtenstein liked all of advertising's techniques: the mechanical dot pattern, the processed look of the color and the imagery, the elementary, "how to draw" images, the banal forms, the consumer products. Advertising represented a synthetic approximation of art; it was this quality that he wanted to convey in his painting. In reacting against Abstract Expressionism, Lichtenstein found a subject he thought "everybody hated." Commercial art was Lichtenstein's way around the impasse presented by action painting, but it also afforded him the means with which to make a statement about form new to painting.

One of Lichtenstein's most effective formal devices was his translation of the benday dot, a mechanical tool of newspaper advertisement, into a formidable painting technique. In his early paintings Lichtenstein used a handmade stencil to screen his dots onto the surface of his canvas. The artist moved the stencil from one area of the painting to another until he had covered its entire surface. Because the dots were hand-painted and the surfaces were irregular, the canvases looked less precise than Lichtenstein would have liked. Nonetheless, to the first-time viewer, the paintings appeared to be reproductions rather than originals. As the artist grew more adept in his technique, he devised a more precise way of replicating the benday dots. Eventually he had the screens manufactured for him. He also began to use the benday dot more effectively in color and in area so that by more recent paintings, such as *Stepping Out* (plate 12), the screen or dot pattern is more autonomous as abstract form and less overt in its reference to its original source in advertising.

One of Lichtenstein's most brilliant achievements was his adaptation of cartoon devices to the demands of painting. *Eddie Diptych* and *Torpedo . . . los!* (plates 6 and 7) are two among many of his works from the early 1960s that feature a heroine engaged in a series of "true romance" dramas and a hero engaged in a series of "world at war" adventures. Both series incorporate the comic-strip balloon and multiple narrative devices as a way of introducing language into the painting. The narrative is one of crisis in both paintings; in these and other works of the period, language sets the stage for action, sound, and movement. The dialogue can be lengthy, as in *Eddie Diptych*, where the unnamed heroine is suffering over her boyfriend "Eddie"; or terse, as when the World War II commander barks out the order, "*Torpedo . . . los*" (Lichtenstein's substitution of Spanish for German adds an element of the ridiculous to the drama of the event), urging his men to bomb the daylights out of the enemy. The call to romance and the call to arms were predictable scenarios to anyone growing up during World War II. Daytime soaps, comic books, and movies emphasized these themes. In his telling paintings of these subjects, Lichtenstein has documented an era as well as a culture. Indeed, they are features of our culture that remain valid to this day.

In 1965 Lichtenstein began a series of paintings of brushstrokes that have been interpreted as a commentary on the New York School of action painting. He has since stated that he wanted to make a statement about the tradition of painting as we know it from the time of the Italian Renaissance. Lichtenstein conceptualized the idea of the bravura brushstroke and rendered it in his usual cool and detached style. As he had done in the cartoons, he first executed paintings like *Yellow and Green Bushstrokes* (plate 8) as small studies which he then enlarged in an opaque projector and redrew on the surface of his canvases. Using this technique to question the mannerisms of painting allowed the artist to recast a stylistic device as his own and to create some of his most ironic and sensuous imagery. Irony and sensuality usually don't go hand-in-hand but they are often paired by Lichtenstein, generally in his choice of subject rather than in his treatment of it. Here the sensuality is achieved by flamboyant form and by the idealization of the act of painting rather than by overt representation. In this respect, his work can be compared with that of Jasper Johns. But the difference is more striking than the similarity, for while Johns often chooses a subject which lends itself to ironic commentary, his painterliness has an autonomous function: it serves both to describe the object and to be about pure painting. Lichtenstein, on the other hand, is unambiguous on the subject of the bravura brushstroke, but as a bravura statement of its own, the brushstroke ironically challenges a painterly tradition by being the very opposite of pure painting. Using means that are completely at odds with those of his predecessors, Lichtenstein employs a limited color palette of blue benday dots, broad strokes of yellow and green outlined in black, and the occasional neat white drip. The notion of making a brushstroke into a concrete form, even to the extent of cleaning up the drips, enabled him to restate in his own language the history of painterliness from Frans Hals to the Abstract Expressionists. Since painterliness is often synonymous with style, *Yellow and Green Brushstrokes* can also be seen as a commentary on the nature of the act of painting. In his transformation of the isolated brushstroke, however, Lichtenstein succeeds in capturing a larger quarry: art itself.

Lichtenstein's modern series was a departure from the familiar subject matter of the comic strip and landscape paintings. The artist chose a subject, the Art Deco architecture and design of the 1920s and 1930s, which was not terribly popular when he began to work with it. (It has become all the rage since.) In his Deco paintings and sculptures he embraced the forms and the ambience of the period: the elaborate theater marquees and stepped façades of buildings in and around Rockefeller Center, the curved brass banisters, ornate carpets, and plush velour stanchion signs in Radio City Music Hall, the overstuffed furniture, automobile grills, and jewelry—the repetitive shapes and geometric patterns. *Preparedness* (plate 9) expresses the sentiment of the 1930s and is, as he has indicated, a call to action, a conspicuous attempt to recover the look of the period and its socio-political message. Lichtenstein notes that he wanted the painting to be a loaded statement about the innocent optimism of the 1930s, such as those that could be found in WPA murals. A triptych, *Preparedness* also extends the concept of the diptych, which was used so effectively in paintings like *Eddie Diptych*. The painting shares with *Eddie Diptych* another similarity; the innocent era of the 1930s was replicated in the 1950s, the era when the cartoon came into its own. Like *Eddie Diptych*, the left-hand panel in *Preparedness* serves to introduce the factory exterior, complete with smokestacks reminiscent of a scene by Charles Demuth. The other two panels depict assembly-line workers busily manufacturing products for a better America. The

painting is set in motion through repetition, the repetition of the factory workers' heads, a feature that is typical of Deco art and design. The painting is also energized, symbolically at least, by emblems of progress, the machinery, the templates, the standardized forms of standard 1930s modernism. Their momentum is reinforced by a striking pattern of diagonals and by the placement of receding forms in space to suggest movement. *Preparedness* refers to the progressive work ethic of 1930s murals, but it also recalls an epic statement on a similar theme, Fernand Léger's *The City*. Lichtenstein's earlier bold painting style had provoked comparisons with Léger, but this is really the first painting of the artist's to lend itself to such a comparison. Lichtenstein found the graphic imagery of Léger's cityscapes intriguing, as his intentions were somewhat similar to that of the French artist. *The City* takes a utopian view of the workers' paradise; *Preparedness* is a comment on, rather than an endorsement of, those beliefs.

Lichtenstein returned to Léger in the late 1970s when he painted *Stepping Out* (plate 12). As in earlier paintings based on or after works by such major modernist artists as Picasso (see plate 7), Léger's art becomes one of the subjects of this painting. In *Stepping Out*, Lichtenstein created an image collaged together from a portion of Léger's *The Country Outing* (1954), with a face derived from one of his own surrealist paintings. He emulates Léger's crisp format, incisive forms, strong contours, and precise palette, but in combining his imagery with that of Léger he created a new dialogue between two artists of different generations. We see Léger through Lichtenstein's eyes and recognize that his appeal to Lichtenstein stems as much from the shared influence of Cubism as from a mutual appreciation of industrialized forms and mechanization.

With paintings such as *Still Life with Goldfish* (plate 10), Lichtenstein began a renewed involvement with still life. Unlike his 1960s still lifes, such as *Black Flowers*, which featured common everyday objects, the still lifes of the 1970s were usually more elaborate and included a complex arrangement of objects, some of them motifs from his earlier work or ornate tableaux in which still life and landscape are merged. *Still Life with Goldfish* is based on Matisse's *Goldfish and Sculpture* (1911), but it also quotes Lichtenstein's own *Golf Ball*. Here, as in many of the still lifes of this period, Lichtenstein manipulated imagery and composition—goldfish, bowl, lemons, a rubber plant, a golf ball, with multiple perspectives—to create a harmonious but implausible setting. In appropriating Matisse's image, Lichtenstein continues to play with the question of originality: the Matisse is itself a highly stylized version of a still life; is the Lichtenstein any less original for being a stylized version of the Matisse?

Among the many subjects that form a cogent part of Lichtenstein's dialogue with art is the Italian twentieth-century Futurist Carlo Carrà's watercolor *The Red Horseman*, of 1913, which formed the basis for the artist's monumental canvas *Red Horseman* (plate 11). Lichtenstein uses an image that symbolized the Futurist movement, especially its fascination with the dynamics of speed and its unequivocal glorification of war. Unlike his earlier cartoons, in which World War II was viewed as a just cause, Lichtenstein's Futurist paintings sidestep the political ramifications of a group of painters who acclaimed war and whose art was later

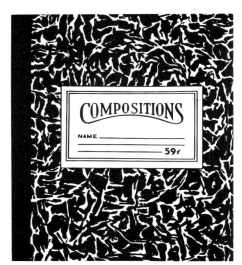

3. *Composition II*. 1964. Magna on canvas, 56 x 48". The Sonnabend Collection, New York

embraced by the fascist state under Mussolini's leadership. From Lichtenstein's point of view, many of the early modern movements, including Futurism, were freighted with social agendas and political manifestos. He thought of Futurism and German Expressionism, for example, as less important offshoots of Cubism. Lichtenstein liked the idea of capturing the look of a movement and divesting it of its political agenda. He wanted to make his work about a movement look like an imitation while at the same time allowing himself enough room to make his own statement. He appropriated the Futurist imagery as a part of his own formal vocabulary and enhanced Carrà's signal Futurist work by completing it. He enlarged its scale, altered its color relationships, and anchored the image to the canvas with a network of intersecting black vectors. In this extraordinary painting one dazzling image recalls the other.

Lichtenstein annexed a series of movements in the 1970s and 1980s, among them the aforementioned Futurism, Surrealism, Cubism, and German Expressionism, each time capturing the essence of the original while putting his own imprint on a style. *Laocoön* (plate 13) is exceptional in the artist's oeuvre in being classical in origin. As such, it joins a few other works, among them *Temple of Apollo* (1964), and *The Great Pyramids* (1969), which are also based upon ancient monuments. While those were created with the idea of commercial reproduction in mind, this painting was done in part as a play upon the notion of sculpture and in part as a statement about expression. To a subject famous for its tormented figures and writhing forms, he has married his Expressionist style. The painting reprises his own late 1950s–early 1960s experiments in Abstract Expressionism and his more recent ventures into German Expressionism. With his sense of irony very much in play, Lichtenstein has elected to propose a subject to the German Expressionists and their American counterparts, the Abstract Expressionists.

By 1991 Lichtenstein had decided to return to originating his imagery. He started a series of interiors, which culminated in such paintings as *Interior with Mirrored Wall* (plate 14). These oversized canvases were usually based upon images taken from the Yellow Pages. As he had in the early 1960s, the artist clipped advertisements of interest to him and made composite room interiors from them. He then made large collages to gain a better understanding of what

the canvases would look like and made slides from them which he projected onto the surface. After redrawing the images on the canvas, he began to map out their contours, tape over the black outlines, lay in the patterns of stripes and dots, and paint in the colors he had chosen. The paintings are varied in subject but all share in common a substantial size, which would appear to invite the viewer to enter the picture. Lichtenstein immediately rendered this notion impossible by juxtaposing portions of a room with other views seen from a different angle. In some instances, he created the reflection of a portion of the room in a bedroom mirror that could not have existed in actuality if the room had been rendered in conventional two-point perspective. In *Still Life with Mirrored Wall*, on the other hand, he presented an interior which seemed straightforward enough, except that it was difficult to discern where the room began and the mirror left off. Lichtenstein's treatment of reflections, his insistence on creating a volume from a void, which had intrigued him from the beginning of his earliest Pop imagery, is one of the most outstanding features of his work. He has treated reflections as they were treated in paintings from the time of the Renaissance, to expand the dimension of the image and bring the spectator into the space of the painting. He has created a dialogue about the nature of reflections in relation to the larger issue of abstraction and used it as an image in his series of mirror paintings. Above all he has enjoyed the notion of playing with volume and void that the mirror suggests and he has handed us this enjoyment for our own delectation.

In these late paintings Lichtenstein is continuing a dialogue he began in his first Pop paintings of 1961. He references artists, indexes subjects, synthesizes styles, and transforms the methods of advertising back into the art forms from which they were originally derived. His consummate understanding of the stylistic developments in our century and his evident skill in appropriating art for his own ends makes it possible for us to better understand our culture and his stunning contribution to art.

NOTES

1. Swenson, G[ene] R. "What is Pop Art?: Answers from 8 Painters, Part I," *ARTnews* 62, no. 7 (November 1963), p. 25. This interview occurred two years after Lichtenstein first exhibited his cartoon imagery. Although his work had more than its share of detractors, by 1963 there was a small but vocal audience for his work, and this prompted the artist to note, "Apparently they didn't hate that [advertising] enough either."
2. Ibid., 1963, p. 25.
3. Conversation with the artist, September 11, 1992.

FURTHER READING

Alloway, Lawrence. *Roy Lichtenstein*. New York: Abbeville Press, 1983.

Busche, Ernst A. *Roy Lichtenstein: Das Frühwerk 1942–1960*. Berlin: Gebr. Mann Verlag, 1988.

Coplans, John. *Roy Lichtenstein*. Pasadena Art Museum, California, in collaboration with the Walker Art Center, Minneapolis. 1967.

Coplans, John, ed. *Roy Lichtenstein*. New York and Washington: Praeger Publications, 1972.

Cowart, Jack *Roy Lichtenstein 1970–1980*. New York: Hudson Hills Press, Inc., in association with the Saint Louis Art Museum, Missouri, 1981.

Hendrickson Janis. *Lichtenstein*. English edition (Danish edition translated by Jannik Storm), Cologne: Benedikt Taschen, 1988.

Hindry, Ann, ed. "Special Issue: Roy Lichtenstein." *Artstudio* 20 (Spring 1991).

Morphet, Richard. *Roy Lichtenstein*. London: The Tate Gallery, 1968.

Rose, Bernice. *The Drawings of Roy Lichtenstein*. New York: The Museum of Modern Art, 1987.

Waldman, Diane. *Roy Lichtenstein*. New York: The Solomon R. Guggenheim Foundation, 1969.

——————. *Roy Lichtenstein*. Milan and New York: Gabriele Mazzotta, 1971 and Harry N. Abrams, Inc., 1972.

——————. *Roy Lichtenstein: Drawings and Prints*. New York: Chelsea House, 1971.

First published in 1993 in the United States of America by
Rizzoli International Publications, Inc.
300 Park Avenue South
New York, New York 10010

Library of Congress Cataloging-in-Publication Data
Roy Lichtenstein/by Diane Waldman.
      p. cm. — (Rizzoli art series)
Includes bibliographical references and index.
ISBN 0–8478–1666–4
1. Lichtenstein, Roy, 1923——Criticism and interpretation.
I. Lichtenstein, Roy, 1923– . II. Title. III. Series.
N6537. L5W36 1993
709.2--dc20   92–36643
                                                          CIP

Complete caption information for colorplate 12: *Stepping Out*. 1978. Oil and magna on canvas, 86 x 70". Collection The Metropolitan Museum of Art, New York. Purchase, Lila Acheson Wallace Gift, Arthur Hoppock Hearn Fund, Arthur Lejwa Fund in honor of Jean Arp, the Bernhil Fund, Joseph H. Hazen Foundation, Inc., Samuel I. Newhouse Foundation, Inc., Walter Bareiss, Marie Bannon McHenry, Louise Smith and Stephen C. Swid Gifts, 1980. (1980.420)

The publisher wishes to acknowledge Shelley Lee for her help with this publication.
Series Editor: Norma Broude
Series designed by José Conde and Betty Lew/Rizzoli

Printed in Italy

Front cover: see colorplate 4

Index to Colorplates

1. *Girl with Ball*. 1961. Oil and magna on canvas, 60¼ x 36¼".
Collection The Museum of Modern Art, New York. Gift of Philip Johnson

2. *Black Flowers*. 1961. Oil on canvas, 70 x 48".
Collection Mr. and Mrs. S. I. Newhouse, Jr.

3. *George Washington*. 1962. Oil on canvas, 51 x 38".
Collection Jean-Christophe Castelli

4. *The Refrigerator*. 1962. Oil on canvas, 68 x 56".
Private Collection

5. *Woman with Flowered Hat*. 1963. Magna on canvas, 50 x 40".
Saatchi Collection, London

6. *Eddie Diptych.* 1962. Oil on canvas, 2 connected panels, 44 x 52".
The Sonnabend Collection, New York

7. *Torpedos. . .los!* 1963. Oil on canvas, 68 x 80".
Private Collection

8. *Yellow and Green Brushstrokes*. 1966. Oil and magna on canvas, 84 x 180".

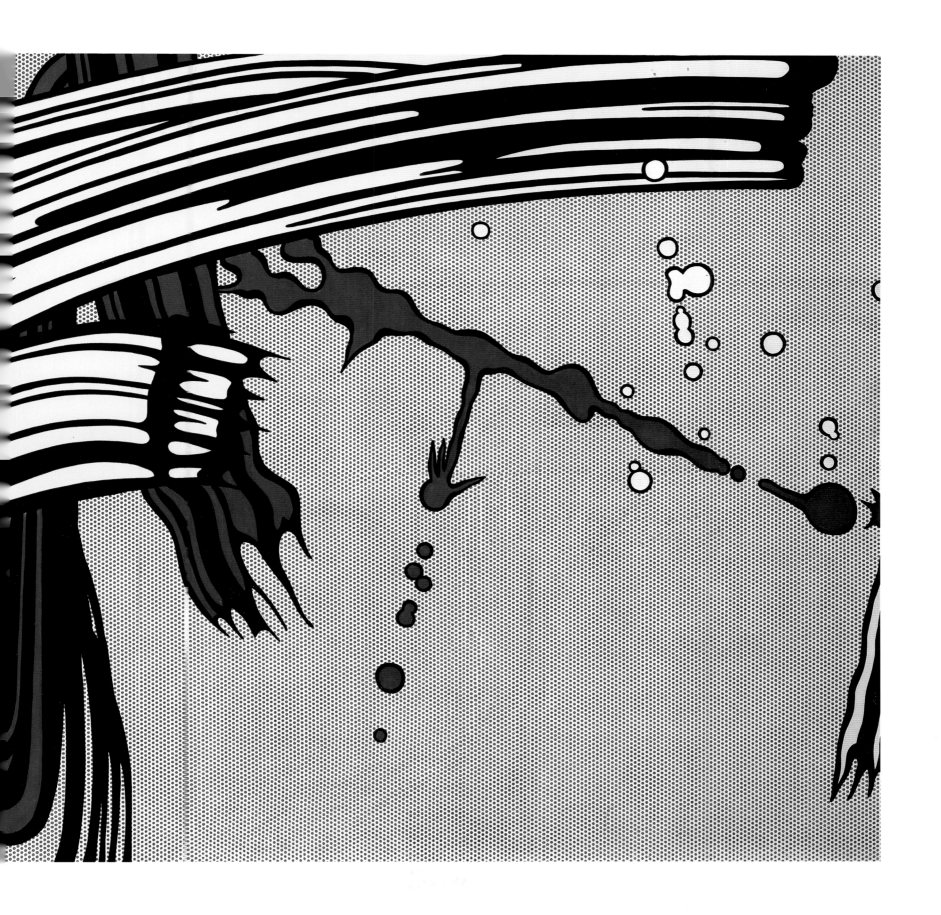

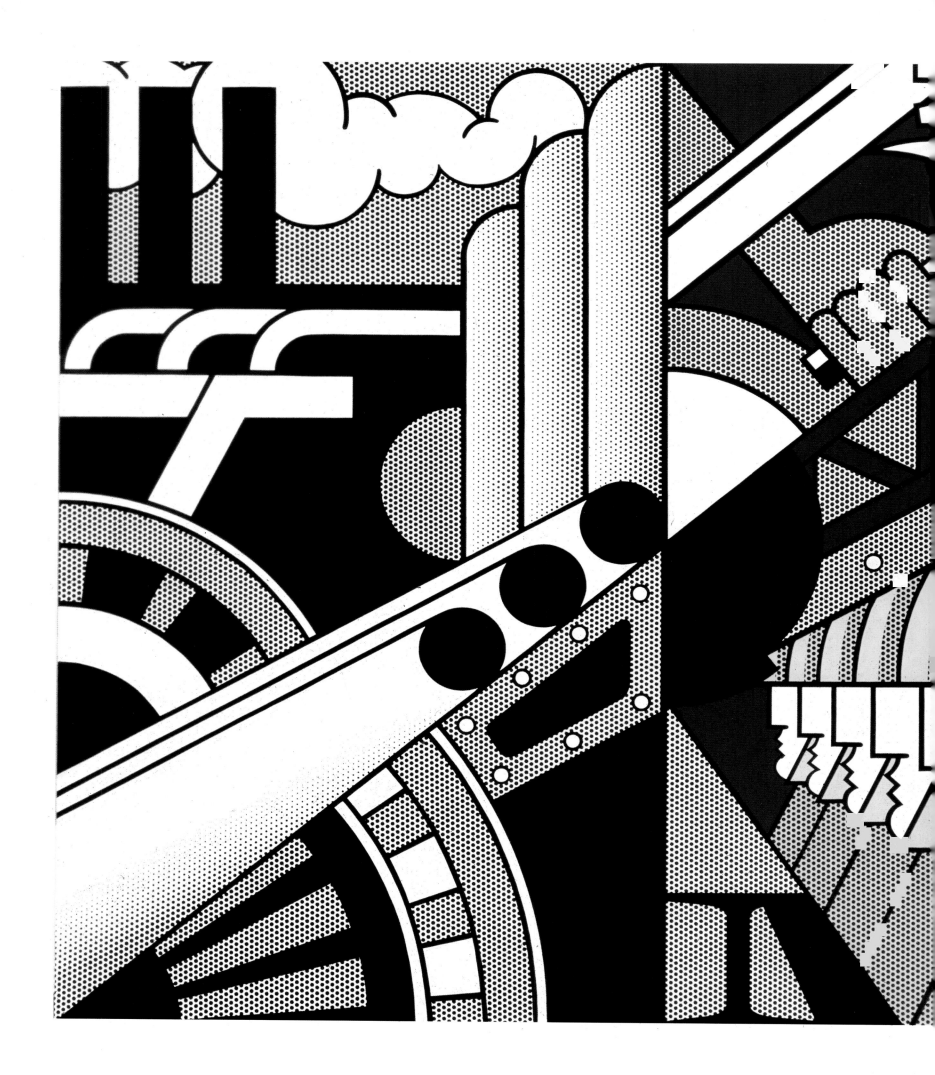

9. *Preparedness*. 1968. Oil and magna on canvas, 3 connected panels, 120 x 216".

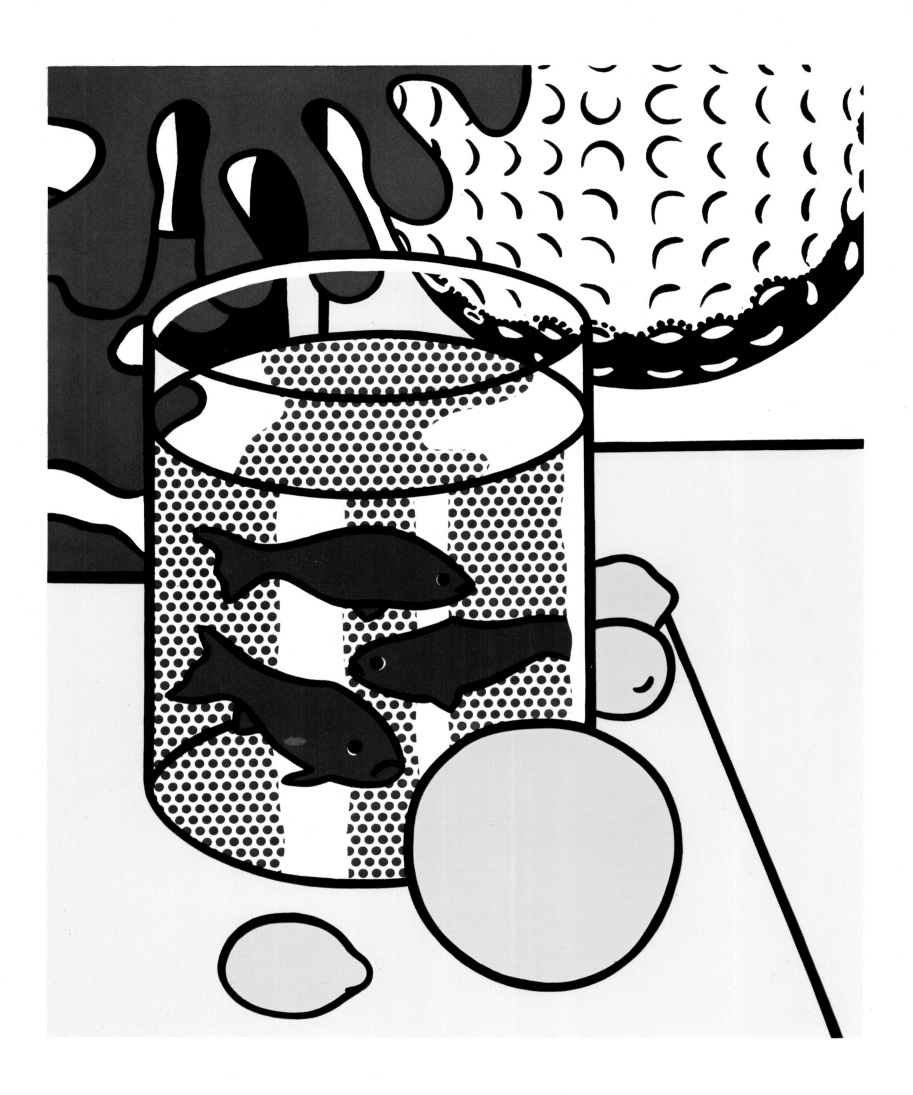

10. *Still Life with Goldfish.* 1972. Oil and magna on canvas, 52 x 42".
Private Collection

11. *Red Horseman.* 1974. Oil and magna on canvas, 84 x 112".
Collection Museum Moderner Kunst Stiftung Ludwig, Vienna

12. *Stepping Out*. 1978. Oil and magna on canvas, 86 x 70". Collection The Metropolitan Museum of Art.
For complete information, see copyright page

11. *Red Horseman.* 1974. Oil and magna on canvas, 84 x 112".
Collection Museum Moderner Kunst Stiftung Ludwig, Vienna

13. *Laocoön*. 1988. Oil and magna on canvas, 120 x 102".
Private Collection

14. *Interior with Mirrored Wall*. 1991. Oil and magna on canvas, 126 x 160".
Collection Solomon R. Guggenheim Museum, New York